THE BRITISH MUSEUM
CHRIST

THE BRITISH MUSEUM
CHRIST

Rowena Loverance

THE BRITISH MUSEUM PRESS

Thanks to Nicholas Holtam for theological insights and advice

Photography by The British Museum Department of Photography
and Imaging and the author

© 2004 The Trustees of The British Museum
First published in 2004 by The British Museum Press
A division of The British Museum Company Ltd
46 Bloomsbury Street, London WC1B 3QQ

Rowena Loverance has asserted her moral right to be identified
as the author of this work
A catalogue record for this book is available from the British Library

ISBN 0 7141 5015-0

Frontispiece: The flight into Egypt, drawing, Taddeo Zuccaro, 1557-59

Extract from 'Little Gidding' by T.S. Eliot reproduced by
kind permission of Faber and Faber Ltd.
Extract from 'Twelfth Night' by Rowan Williams reproduced
by kind permission of Lambeth Palace.

Designed and typeset in Centaur by Peter Ward
Printed in China by C&C Offset

CONTENTS

INTRODUCTION

ENCOUNTERING CHRIST

Many millions of people through the last two millennia have had a personal encounter with Christ. A few hundred people in first-century Palestine met Jesus of Nazareth; a vastly greater number believe they have encountered the living person of Jesus after his death. The term Christ, Greek *Christos*, is a translation of the Hebrew *Meshiah*, Messiah, and means 'the anointed one'; it is used in Christianity as a title for Jesus and to distinguish the Jesus of history from the Christ of faith.

On this enamel jewel, across differences of gender and religious affiliation, Jesus is talking to a woman from non-Jewish Samaria. His request for a drink leads to a conversation about water, but they're really talking about life. He somehow diagnoses her chequered marital history; she says afterwards 'He told me everything I ever did'. She tells him that she knows the Messiah, the Christ, is coming, and he replies: 'I, who speak to you, am he' (John 4.26).

A fashionable piece of male jewellery like a hat badge may seem a frivolous place to find such a statement of faith. But the text is in English, from the middle years of the Reformation: the badge is making a further statement that God does not have to be mediated through a Latin-speaking clergy, but can be met directly by every man and woman.

Enamel, England, 16th century

CHRISTENDOM

Based on their experience of personal response, the followers of Jesus constructed a theology and a religion. It seemed to them that for Jesus to have the life and power which those who knew him had felt, he must not only have a deep understanding of God, but must in some sense be God. Through a process of councils and controversies, heresies and heterodoxies, most Christians came to agree that Jesus was both fully man and fully God, the creator and sustainer of the universe.

Was Christianity to be a religion of power or of protest? This is one of the earliest known representations of Christ; it comes from the dining-room floor of a wealthy villa-owner in Dorset, when the prosperity of Roman Britain was at its height. Christ is shown as a Roman emperor, with heavy features and a severely-cut fringe, and appears to be wearing a Roman toga. The mosaicist has set this image, which he may have taken from a head on a coin, against a background of pomegranates, a symbol of eternal life from ancient Greece, and the new-style *chi-rho*, Greek letters meaning *Christos*.

The conversion of the emperor Constantine to Christianity in AD 312 represented the first and most significant of Christianity's accommodations with secular authority. The emperor gained control over the church, the right to convene its councils, influence the appointment of its bishops and resolve its heresies; the church gained the immense but questionable advantage of identification with power. 'Christendom', the resulting marriage of church and state, has taken many forms, in medieval western Europe, Orthodox Byzantium and Tsarist Russia; even in today's multi-cultural societies, its lure has not been entirely dispelled.

Floor mosaic, Hinton St Mary, Dorset, 4th century

GLOBAL CHRISTIANITY

Christ told his followers to spread the gospel – the good news – and Christianity became and has remained a missionary faith. Its theology and visual imagery were formed by contact with its immediate neighbours, Judaism and the Graeco-Roman world; and as it spread beyond Europe, to Africa, Asia and America, it encountered different indigenous religions, pre-existing world religions such as Zoroastrianism, Hinduism and Buddhism, and its own younger sibling, Islam, the third 'religion of the book'. Christianity showed remarkable flexibility in adapting to these different religious circumstances.

Christianity reached China along the Silk Road in the seventh century. These Christians were Nestorians, followers of a fifth-century heresy which maintained the separation of the human and divine natures of Christ. They had fled eastward to avoid persecution. This painted silk comes from a collection of mainly Buddhist paintings on silk and paper found in a cave near the oasis town of Dunhuang. The figure, presumably of a Christian worshipper, wears a cross in his headdress, shown in the Nestorian 'floral' version which depicts the cross as a symbol of triumph and regeneration rather than of suffering. But in his hand he holds a flower between two fingers in a pose more characteristic of Buddhist donor figures and *bodhisattvas* on their way to enlightenment.

Silk fragment, from cave 17, Mogao,
near Dunhuang, Gansu province, China, 9th century

POST-CHRISTIANITY?

One of the characteristics of a post-Christian world is the individualization of religion, or as many now prefer to call it, spirituality. For Christianity, which requires both individual and communal expression, this has led in the West at least to a period of rapid decline.

This trend has also encouraged people to select the parts of the faith which appeal to their own life-style. This mass-produced medal encourages two early twentieth-century French motorists to travel safely by contemplating St. Christopher. St Christopher became the patron saint of travellers because the main story told about him, from the fifth century, was that he carried the Christ child across a river. He is now thought not to have been a historical character, and was demoted from sainthood by the Catholic Church in 1969. But for the kind of spirituality which flourishes in tokens and talismans, this has hardly diminished his popularity.

Although the retreat of institutional Christianity means that Christian artefacts of the kind featured here are no longer being widely produced, contemporary artists such as Craigie Aitchison, Bill Viola and Mark Wallinger are re-engaging with Christianity's core material to create original works of art. Artists and theologians alike have to decide whether Christianity can best be revived by concentrating on the faith as it was revealed, or whether it needs to be reinterpreted and revisualized for today's generation. Like other revealed religions, Christianity seeks an answer to this dilemma.

Metal-alloy, France, early 20th century

Pen drawing of Bethlehem by Jan van Scorel, probably drawn in 1520.
On the left is the Convent of the Nativity where, according to tradition,
Jesus was born.

LIFE

JESUS' CONCEPTION

The first human response to Christ, which sets the events of his life in motion, is that of Mary, an unmarried girl living in Nazareth, a village near Sepphoris in Palestine. Mary's willing acceptance of the unexpected message, delivered via the angel Gabriel, that through the power of God she is to have a child, opens up the channel for God's direct intervention in the human story through the birth of Jesus.

This is a very appropriate story to show on an embroidered panel because in Annunciation scenes Mary is often depicted spinning or weaving. Partly this is simply a traditional female activity, but stories also grew up that Mary spent her early life in the Jewish Temple, so she is often shown weaving a new curtain for it; this also anticipates the idea that Jesus through his death will tear the veil of the Temple apart. Embroidery is a luxury art – it was time-consuming to produce, and rich pieces like this use silver-gilt thread as well as coloured silks. This panel is probably from the cuffs or hem of an alb, the undergarment worn by a priest when celebrating the eucharist, the central ritual of Christian worship. English embroidery was highly prized and widely exported in the Middle Ages.

Embroidery, found in Spain, woven in England, 14th century

BIRTH

Nine months on, due to the bureaucratic demands of the Roman emperor Augustus, Mary and her husband Joseph were registering for the census in their ancestral town of Bethlehem. Unable to get home in time for the birth, they made do with what accommodation they could find. The gospel writer Luke tells of the baby being placed in a manger; western artists tend to locate this in a stable, while artists from the eastern church thought a cave was more expressive of the rocky landscape of Palestine – as well as foreshadowing the cave of Christ's burial. In Christianity beginnings often foreshadow endings, just as endings can be new beginnings, and Christians refer to Christ as both alpha and omega, in the Greek alphabet the beginning and the end.

The Greek word for this scene, *genesis*, beginning, shown in the top right of the ivory plaque, firmly states the Christian belief that with the birth of Jesus, the human story is beginning all over again, but this time in a higher gear, with God directly revealed to us through Jesus' earthly life. The Byzantine artist has adopted a 'time-lapse' approach to the gospel and later apocryphal accounts, so that three episodes following the birth itself – placing the baby in the manger, the angels' annunciation to the shepherds and Jesus' first bath – are all shown simultaneously. The narrative story and its theological meaning are combined.

Ivory, Constantinople (modern Istanbul, Turkey), 10th century

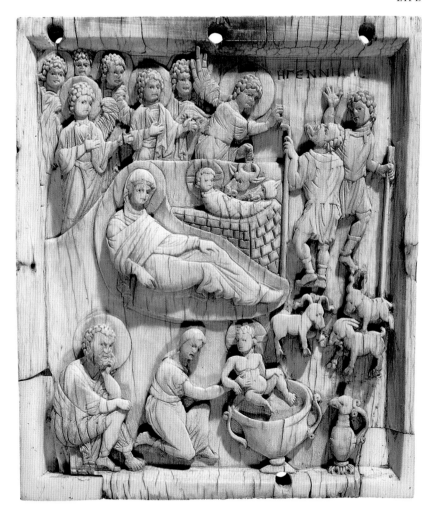

EASTERN PROMISES

Two of the three kings who, according to the gospel writer Matthew, were Jesus' next visitors, are shown on this panel by the prolific Gothic wood sculptor, Tilman Riemenschneider. The third king probably appeared on an adjacent panel, the whole being part of an altarpiece for a church in southern Germany, just before the outbreak of the Reformation.

Matthew actually describes them as *Magi* from the east, perhaps Zoroastrian priests from Iran; they introduce an exotic element into the story and begin to indicate that God's message in Christ is not just for Jewish people but for everyone. Their gifts – gold, frankincense and myrrh – foreshadow the embalming of Christ's body for the tomb, as well as referring to the earthly wealth which he was to shun. Gradually, as they come to represent the whole of mankind, they are shown as men of different ages and from different parts of the world – from the sixteenth-century age of discovery onwards, one of them is usually shown as black.

Christ's appearance, *epiphany* in Greek, to the Magi is celebrated by Christians on Twelfth Night, the title of a poem by Rowan Williams:

> Journeys for old men are not kind
> when comfort's sold to buy the single pearl;
> yet the child's eye is lifetime's worth of gold,
> world's worth of pilgrimage

Limewood, southern Germany, early 16th century

ASYLUM-SEEKER AND REFUGEE

Soon after Jesus' birth, Joseph fled with his family to Egypt. Alerted to a potential danger by the eastern strangers, Herod the Great, the powerful king of Palestine and client of the Roman Empire, had ordered that all boys aged two and under in the Bethlehem district should be rounded up and killed. When Herod's death and the break-up of his kingdom allowed them to return to Palestine, Jesus as a young boy was repeating the Exodus journey, a founding experience of the Jewish people.

Once back in Palestine, the gospel writers offer few clues to Jesus' childhood, and apocryphal legends grew up to fill the gap. The stories so vividly illustrated on these inlaid wall tiles point up in homely terms the problems of growing up alongside a boy with miraculous powers. Playing on the banks of the Jordan, Jesus makes some pools of water which his playmate then knocks down; Jesus gets cross and strikes him dead. Mary remonstrates with him, so Jesus restores the boy to life. Not surprisingly, later scenes show parents' reluctance to let their children play with Jesus at all. They lock them away in towers or ovens to keep them out of harm's way and Jesus then has to come to their rescue.

These tiles also remind us of the parallels between the largely agricultural societies of first-century Palestine and fourteenth-century England. Though Jesus used many farming analogies in his ministry, the gospel writers suggest that when he grew up he became a craftsman, a carpenter like Joseph. Beyond that, nothing of his daily life is known.

Ceramic, Tring, Hertfordshire, early 14th century

DISCOVERING A VOCATION

A voice cries in the wilderness
Prepare the way for the Lord
Clear a straight path for him

Isaiah, 40.3

Only when he is about thirty does Jesus emerge on to the public stage and the main pages of the gospel writers. The setting is still the banks of the Jordan, where a prophet, John, is baptizing people in the river as a symbol of their repentance and the forgiveness of their sins. Jesus comes forward for baptism, and is recognized by John as a greater figure than he, who will baptize people not with water, but with the Spirit of God. Like the Annunciation to Mary, this is a moment when someone else recognizes God as active in the human story. John sees the Spirit of God like a dove coming to rest on Jesus. This is the start of Jesus' mission, to proclaim the good news that the kingdom of God, the promise of social justice and personal transformation, is a present reality, here and now.

Matthew appears embarrassed that Jesus accepted baptism when presumably he had no sins to repent, which rather supports the historical veracity of this particular gospel passage. John is Jesus' cousin and the two are almost the same age, but the Anglo-Saxon artist of this walrus ivory panel shows John the Baptist as an older, bearded man, baptizing the young Christ. He has also transformed John's rough camel hair garments into an elegant arrangement of pleats and folds. The dove is missing but the agitated waters of the Jordan give dynamism to this scene of the start of Jesus' ministry.

Walrus ivory, England, 10th century

FISHERS OF MEN

After his baptism, the gospel writers record that Jesus spent some time alone, wrestling with various temptations towards self-dramatization in the conduct of his public career. Overcoming these, he went back to his home town of Nazareth and its surroundings to start his ministry, preaching in the synagogues and reading aloud from the Hebrew Bible. But he soon sees the need for fellow-workers, and he finds the first of these among the fishing community on Lake Galilee. Simon, one of the fishermen, has had a bad night and caught nothing; putting to sea again at Jesus' suggestion he makes a huge catch. With his brother Andrew and their neighbours James and John, they become Jesus' first disciples.

The calling of the disciples also demonstrates that Jesus has a sense of humour. When he calls Nathaniel by name, and Nathaniel queries how he knows him, Jesus replies that he has seen him under a fig tree. Nathaniel thereupon expresses his belief in Jesus: 'You are the son of God, the king of Israel', to which Jesus replies 'You're saying this just because I said I saw you under a fig tree. You'll see greater things than that!'

Simon was to become known as Cephas or Peter, the rock, the leader of the disciples. All four sides of this carved stone capital from the Cluniac priory at Lewes, in Sussex, are decorated with scenes relating to Peter's life. Cluny, in Burgundy, was founded during the monastic reform movement of the tenth century and this daughter house was under the special protection of the Pope.

Stone, Lewes Priory, Sussex, 13th century

POWER OVER THE ELEMENTS

This ninth-century Carolingian ivory suggests a splendid setting for Christ's first miracle, in a fine building with columned porticos, tied-back curtains and huge spiral-fluted amphorae. It reflects the setting in which the gospel-book it contained would have been used, the court of the French king Charles the Bald, for whom the book's scribe, Liuthard, is known to have produced three manuscripts.

We know much less about the original setting, in Cana in Galilee. There was a wedding, the wine ran out, and John's account reads almost as if Jesus' proud mother egged him on into performing a miracle, turning the water in the huge stone jars into wine. But the punch line, that most people save their poor wine until the guests are too drunk to notice, 'but you have kept the best till last', strikes a very human touch.

Several of Jesus' miracles fall into the category of power over the elements. On one level it may seem that he is succumbing to the first of the temptations he was supposed to have resisted, to turn stones into bread; so some modern writers have tried to argue them away, suggesting for instance that he created vast amounts of food from a few loaves and fishes by persuading people to share their sandwiches. But for God, the creator and sustainer of the world, such actions would be a natural expression of his being.

Ivory, France, 9th century

28

HEALING OF MIND AND BODY

Jesus' ministry drew large crowds, attracted especially by his healing miracles. He healed people bowed down by physical illnesses and disabilities: a man outcast by leprosy, a woman who had been haemorrhaging blood for twelve years. Many of the accounts seem to describe people with mental illness: a girl tormented by a devil, two men possessed by demons, living in a cemetery and terrorizing the neighbourhood. In many cases we are told that he gave strict instructions that the healed were to be silent about their cures, but that was asking rather a lot of human nature, and word continued to spread.

In this scene Rembrandt has captured several of the strands of Jesus' ministry. The setting is beyond the Jordan, where crowds have followed him. Among them are the Pharisees, the religious proselytizers of their day, apparently trying as usual to set verbal traps for him. The disciples, meanwhile, are attempting to hold the crowd at bay. But Jesus corrects them in a phrase which has come down to us laden with sentimentality 'Suffer the little children'. This is actually a huge challenge to all our ideas about growing up, and what it is that constitutes maturity: 'Whoever does not accept the kingdom of God like a child will never enter it'.

Christ healing the sick, etching, Rembrandt van Rijn, Netherlands, 1647

GOD AS LIGHT

Jesus preached the imminent coming of the kingdom of God, and the gospels contain a revelation of how Jesus might appear in that kingdom, when his divine nature would be clearly seen. While Jesus was at prayer on a hillside one evening, Peter, James and John saw him transfigured in a blaze of light; they watched him talking with Moses, the great law-giver, and Elijah, foremost among the Jewish prophets; they heard God's voice telling them 'This is my Son, listen to him'.

This icon combines the scene of the Transfiguration with three earlier times in Jesus' life when God's purpose broke through into this world, his conception, birth and baptism. It was probably painted in northern Greece in the early fourteenth century, a time when Orthodox monks on Mt Athos were in the grip of the revival known as *Hesychasm*, silence, a belief in the unknowability of God. Light, one of the expressions of God's energy, was thus one way in which he could be known.

The Transfiguration, commemorated on 6 August in the western church, is now indissoluably linked to the dropping of the atom bomb on Hiroshima. Humanity is disfigured, but it can also be transfigured by its response to the divine. This scene is placed in the gospels just before Jesus leaves Galilee for Jerusalem, and is full of foreboding. Using a term by which he often referred to himself, Jesus spoke of the coming time when 'the Son of Man will suffer at their hands'.

Icon, from Constantinople (modern Istanbul, Turkey)
or Thessaloniki, northern Greece, early 14th century

ΠΕΤ

ΜΟΡΦΟ
CIC

THE LAST MEAL TOGETHER

The last thing Jesus did as a free man before his imprisonment and trial was to eat with his friends. He was in Jerusalem for the Jewish Passover, and this was the main meal of the festival. With him were the twelve men, his disciples or apostles, whom he had chosen from his wider group of followers to carry on his work. It was from this meal that Judas, one of the twelve, left to betray Jesus' whereabouts to the priests who wanted to try him for blasphemy.

Sets of apostle spoons like these, each one modelled with a figure of one of the apostles, commemorate what came to be known as the Last Supper. Such spoons were popular in Protestant northern Europe; they were used for dining, rather than for any directly religious purpose. This is one of only two complete sets by a single maker to have survived from early Tudor England; it dates from 1536-7, a key year in the English Reformation.

When Jesus shared wine and broke bread with his friends at the Passover meal, the words he spoke foretelling the coming of God's kingdom and identifying the food and drink with his own body and blood, soon to be broken and shed have, in their re-enactment, become the act of worship which creates and binds the Christian community.

Silver, London, 1535-7

TORTURE AND BETRAYAL

Once Judas had betrayed Jesus to the priests, who found him guilty of blasphemy, they brought him before the secular official, the governor of the new Roman province of Judaea, Pontius Pilate. Pilate was unimpressed by the charge, but yielded to the demands of the mob which the priests had whipped up. Matthew describes him washing his hands in full view of the crowd to show that he was not responsible for Jesus' death.

Jesus' friends deserted him, as he had foretold they would. Peter, who had repeatedly vowed to stand firm, sat with the crowd round a fire in the high priest's courtyard, and three times denied that he knew Jesus. Jesus had previously told Peter that he would do so, 'tonight, before the cock crows'.

Jesus was sent for crucifixion, the Roman punishment for political or religious agitation, dragging the crossbeam of his own cross along the road to Mt Calvary.

This ivory telescopes these three scenes with all their narrative detail into a width of less than ten centimetres. It is the first of four panels which together tell the whole Passion story; they are in extremely high relief and must have decorated the sides of a small box, but its purpose is not known. The date of the plaques, around 420, places them at the very beginning of the development of Christian iconography.

Ivory, 4th century, Rome

CRUCIFIXION

The theme of personal encounter with Christ holds up till the very end of his life. Amid the squalor of the horrific event, the row of crosses at Golgotha, the mocking crowd and the soldiers dicing for Jesus' abandoned clothes, the gospel writers maintain the fabric of human relationships. Jesus promises one of his fellow-sufferers that they will meet again in paradise, the officiating Roman centurion recognizes a divine quality in Jesus' death, and a new relationship is created between Jesus' mother Mary and the disciple John, as they stand together beneath the Cross. And we see more clearly than ever Jesus' relationship with God: his response, during the three hours he took to die, moves full circle from abandonment to acceptance.

Some Crucifixion scenes magnify its horror and chaos, but this engraved rock-crystal concentrates sparingly on its essentials. The beauty of the raw material conveys the contrasting light and dark of the scene: the Virgin and St John are the human mourners, the sun and moon are global witnesses, the snake wrapped round the Cross reminds us of the purpose of the Crucifixion, to redeem humankind from Adam's fall.

This celebrated object was made in the court circle of Charles the Bald in the mid-9th century, and was re-used 300 years later by Suger, the abbot of the royal monastery of St. Denys in Paris. When Suger translated the saint's relics into his new abbey church in 1144, he set the rock-crystal as a jewel in the tabernacle.

Rock-crystal, France, 9th century

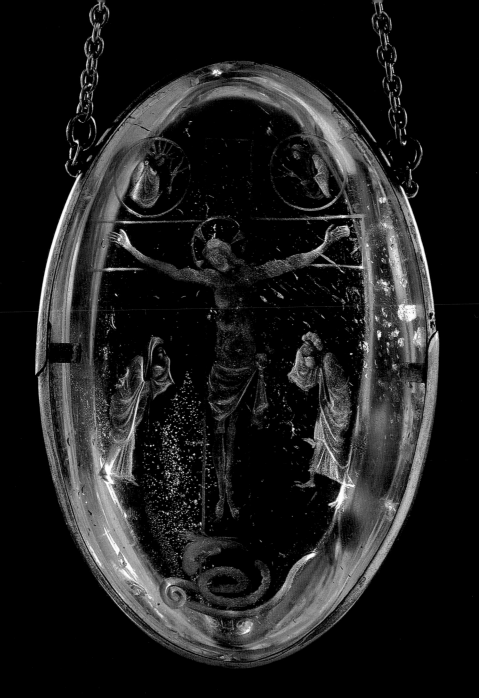

RESURRECTION

Unlike most of his male disciples, the women in Jesus' life had stayed to the bitter end of the Crucifixion and continued to tend his body. It was on the third day that one of them, Mary of Magdala, saw that the stone at the entry to the tomb had been moved, and the body was missing. As she stood there crying, she saw someone she took to be the gardener, but when he spoke to her by name, she recognized him as Jesus. She went back to tell the others 'I have seen the Lord'.

The gospels witness to the empty tomb rather than the actual Resurrection, as do the earliest visualizations of the scene. In the eastern church artists developed a version of *Anastasis*, Resurrection, which imagines Christ descending into Hell and raising the dead, the so-called Harrowing of Hell. From the later Middle Ages, however, especially in the western church, artists have tried to visualize the actual moment of Christ's Resurrection.

Alabaster, quarried in south Derbyshire and Nottinghamshire and carved into high-relief panels, was England's main artistic export in the fourteenth and fifteenth centuries; some 2000 examples survive, from Croatia to Iceland. This version of the Resurrection was one of their most popular subjects; following perhaps the text of the Chester mystery play, it shows Christ rising bodily from the tomb, stepping out on to a moustachioed Roman soldier in fifteenth-century armour, with pointed bassinet and tippet of mail. Christ carries the jewelled cross and Resurrection banner of victory.

Alabaster, England, 15th century

SEEING IS BELIEVING

The appearance of the risen Christ to Mary of Magdala was the beginning of several such reunions. These experiences often echo moments of encounter in Jesus' earthly life: the disciples walking to Emmaus recognize him when he breaks bread with them, Peter recognizes him beside the lake after another miraculously heavy catch.

Back in Jerusalem, Jesus appears to a roomful of the disciples, but Thomas is absent, and expresses incredulity that such a thing could possibly have happened: 'Unless I put my finger into the place where the nails were, I will never believe it'. A week later the experience is repeated. This time Thomas is present and is convinced, but as Jesus points out: 'You have found faith because you have seen me. Happy are those who find faith without seeing me.'

This pewter pilgrim flask has an image of the women at the empty tomb on one side and Thomas' moment of belief on the other. It was used for bringing sacred oil or water from a holy site, a common practice in the sixth and seventh centuries in the period of pilgrimage to the Holy Land before the Arab invasions. But various details suggest that this flask may be of later date, perhaps from the Crusader period. The Greek text on one side says 'Blessing of the Lord from the Holy Places' and on the other Thomas' statement of faith: 'My Lord and My God' (John 20.28).

Pewter, found in Egypt, originally from the Holy Land, 11th-13th century

BEYOND SIGHT AND TOUCH

Christ's post-Resurrection appearances are the culminating episodes in the gospel accounts. Their conclusion, when Christ's physical presence withdraws from the disciples, is told as the first episode in the Acts of the Apostles, generally considered to be another work of the gospel writer Luke.

The text describes him as lifted up before their very eyes, until a cloud hides him from their sight. The scene is generally visualized with Christ ascending vertically into heaven; sometimes just his feet appear dangling from the upper frame. In this gold medallion, he appears enthroned in an oval mandorla, a way of indicating that he is present outside time. The mandorla is carried by two angels, and above it appear two of the four living creatures – ox, lion, eagle and man – described in the Book of Revelation as surrounding the throne of God.

Thirteen characters are shown at ground level. One is clearly Christ himself, bearing the cross; the rest are the disciples, probably with Paul, who became a disciple only after Christ's death, replacing the traitor Judas. Other versions of the scene sometimes add in Mary, though she is not mentioned as present in the text. The text on this medallion is also unusual, referring back to Jesus' words at the Last Supper, 'Our peace we leave with you'. (John 14.27).

Gold, probably from the Holy Land, 6th or early 7th century

THE ERUPTION OF GOD

Jesus promised his disciples that after his death they would come to know the Holy Spirit of God as their advocate and comforter. This experience bursts upon them at Hag Shavuot or Pentecost, the Jewish harvest festival. The Acts of the Apostles describes a strong driving wind and flames like tongues of fire, but Christian artists, drawing on the imagery of Christ's baptism, usually portray a dove.

The infant faith of Christianity now explodes beyond those who actually knew Jesus. Jerusalem is crowded with Jews from all over the Roman world, who each hear the gospel in their own language. Whereas the story of the Tower of Babel in the Old Testament illustrates the fracturing of language, Pentecost shows that human beings can communicate beyond language with one another and with God. God pours out his spirit on all humankind.

There is no record of the Virgin Mary at Pentecost, but in the western tradition she becomes a key presence. This fifteenth-century Book of Hours, a collection of liturgical texts, belonged to Jacob de Brégilles, a leading nobleman at the court of Philip the Good of Burgundy. The miniatures are in *grisaille*, grey-toned, and the borders are inhabited by all kinds of animals, humans and birds.

> The dove descending breaks the air
> With flame of incandescent terror
> Of which the tongues declare
> The one discharge from sin and error.
> The only hope, or else despair
>   Lies in the choice of pyre or pyre —
>   To be redeemed from fire by fire
>
> *Little Gidding*, T.S. ELIOT

Manuscript, Bruges, southern Netherlands, around 1460

BELIEFS

DRAWING ON JEWISH TRADITION

The first Jewish Christians, as they re-assessed their existing beliefs and their new experiences, naturally turned to the Hebrew Bible and re-read it in the light of Christ's life. It seemed to them that many prophetic passages had now found their resolution, and that even descriptive passages could foreshadow events in Christ's life. This idea of seeing 'types' of Christ in what Christians now called the Old Testament was to become basic to Christian theology and art.

This enamel cross from the Meuse (Mosan) region of Belgium, which probably served as a reliquary for fragments of the Cross, shows the level of detail these ideas had reached by the twelfth century.

Some scenes are purely visual allusions: in the centre, Jacob crosses his hands to bless Joseph's sons Ephraim and Manasseh, while on the left, the widow of Sarepta who cooked for Elijah holds her two sticks in the form of a cross. Others, though, are more theological: the brazen serpent, in the top panel, which Moses and Aaron set up on a standard in the desert to save the people from snake bite was an obvious type of Christ's saving role on the Cross; on the right the slaughtered lamb of the original Passover prefigures Christ's sacrifice, while on the bottom panel the grapes which spies brought back to the people of Israel from Canaan, the Promised Land, refer through the Last Supper to Christ's blood.

Previous page: Floor mosaic with Christian symbols and inscriptions, 5th century, House of Eustolios, Kourion, Cyprus

Enamel, France or Belgium, 12th century

DRAWING ON THE CLASSICAL TRADITION

As Christianity spread to Greece and Rome through the missionary activity of St Paul, these new converts tried to find the same kind of prefiguring in the classical tradition as Jewish converts did in the Old Testament. Heroes defeating monsters became Christ overcoming the powers of evil; Christ himself came to be visualized as a Roman emperor (p.8). Virgil's pastoral poetry anticipated Christ's kingdom on earth, and Orpheus calming the animals stood for Christ in the peaceable kingdom prophesied by Isaiah.

The classical sibyls, priestesses at the oracle sites of the ancient world, also came in for this Christian treatment. If they were prophets, it was reasoned, they must have foretold the coming of Christ. So the most renowned classical sibyl, from Cumæ in Italy, was believed to have prophesied the Nativity, while the Delphic sibyl from Greece prophesied the Crucifixion, holding as her attribute a crown of thorns. Twelve sibyls were 'typecast' in this way: this rather less well-known sibyl from Europe holds a sword to symbolize Herod's Massacre of the Innocents.

These twelve plaques come from Limoges, in central France, famous for its champlevé enamels in the twelfth century and again for its painted enamels in the sixteenth century. Léonard Limousin, whose initials appear on the sword, worked at the French court for Francis I and Henry II. Sadly, the sword also serves to foreshadow the bitter French Wars of Religion, which broke out in the following reign.

Enamel, France, 16th century

THE VIRGIN BIRTH

The core belief about Jesus is that he is 'God with us', 'The Word made flesh'. This is illustrated from the very beginning of the gospel accounts by emphasizing that Jesus was the son of Mary, but not of Joseph. He did not have an earthly father: 'It is through the Holy Spirit that she has conceived' (Matthew 2.20).

The whalebone casket known as the Franks Casket is a fascinating historical document because it gives us an insight into the beliefs and world view of people newly converted to Christianity. It comes from Northumbria about AD 700, that is within a century or so of the Anglo-Saxon conversion. It is decorated with several narrative scenes, though this double scene on the front is the only one with a Christian theme. It directly relates the Christian story of the Nativity to an Anglo-Saxon story – the rape of Beaudohild by Wayland the Smith – often believed to be one of the manifestations of the Norse god Odin. So both scenes present a woman bearing a child without an earthly father; both sons went on to live heroic but ultimately tragic lives. A surviving Anglo-Saxon poem, which also refers to this story, doesn't seek to minimize the catastrophe, which throws an unusual light on the usual Christian understanding of the Virgin Birth:

'Her womb grew great with child
When she knew that, she could never hold
Steady before her wit what was to happen.
  That went by, this will too'

Whalebone, probably from Northumbria, England, early 8th century

ONLY SON OF GOD

O f all the beliefs about Christ, the most problematic one in today's multicultural world is that he is unique, the only complete revelation of God, relating to God like an only son to his father. This is implicit in the gospel accounts and becomes explicit in the church's credal formulations of the fourth century.

In this engraving the seventeenth-century French artist, Claude Mellon, has found his own unique way of visualizing this. He has drawn the face of Christ, and indeed the whole plate, in a single unbroken line from the tip of Jesus' nose, achieving the colouring by varying the thickness of the line. This version of Christ's face, known as *The Sudarium* or *Veil of St. Veronica*, reflects the legend that when a woman wiped Christ's sweating face as he struggled to carry the Cross, the image of his features was miraculously transferred onto her cloth. A similar story, told of a cloth with Christ's image sent in his lifetime to King Abgar of Edessa, may lie behind the later forgery of the Turin Shroud.

The text, *Formatus Unicus Una*, the one formed in one, is a pun on the three aspects of uniqueness: engraving, veil and incarnation.

As Christianity spread and encountered older world faiths, Christians have had to decide whether to assert this traditional view, the so-called scandal of particularity, or to moderate their claims, viewing the Christian revelation as one of several ways through which humanity communicates with the divine.

The Sudarium or *Veil of St Veronica*, engraving, Claude Mellan, France, 1649

FORMATVR VNICVS VNA

ONE PERSON OF THE TRINITY

From a twentyfirst-century global perspective, the debates within Christianity about Christ's role, his relationship to God and how best to worship him, can seem rather parochial. Ecumenical dialogue between the Christian traditions has a long history, but has usually been a minority interest, and has left little mark on Christian art.

One striking exception is the Trinity medal, the silver masterpiece of Hans Reinhart the Elder of Leipzig, Germany. Reinhart was a cabinet-maker by training, who briefly flowered as a silversmith, making twenty-six signed portrait and biblical medals in eight years. He worked for the Protestant duke of Saxony within the Holy Roman Empire ruled by a Catholic emperor. The medal takes as its starting point the text of the Athanasian Creed, the first lines of which appear on the back, and which even at the height of the Reformation represented a continuing point of agreement between the Catholic and Protestant churches.

The invocation of God as Father, Son and Holy Spirit in the Creed is given visual form in the high relief casting on the front, with God seated in Majesty, the crucified Christ and the Holy Spirit as a dove. Though the Trinity is not specifically mentioned in the gospel accounts, Christians from the first century onwards came to define their faith in the three persons of God: God as Creator, Jesus as Redeemer and Holy Spirit as Sustainer. In our own time this understanding of the complex nature of God, with different personas interrelating one to another, carries renewed psychological conviction.

Silver, Germany, 1544

TRIUMPH OVER EVIL

'Salt is good, but if salt itself becomes tasteless, how will it be seasoned? It is useless; it can only be thrown away!' (Luke 14.34). This object has been known as a salt-cellar since the nineteenth century, though they had not yet been invented when it was made in the fifteenth century. This group of ivories came out of the meeting of two cultures: Christian Portuguese traders and the Sapi peoples of West Africa, present-day Sierra Leone. Made by the locals as tourist souvenirs, they are based on European shapes, but their figural decoration is entirely African. African symbols of royalty sit alongside Portuguese heraldry; this one is unusual in being composed entirely of European motifs.

These first encounters were of limited missionary success. An African bishop of West Africa was appointed, but the missions seem to have died out by the mid-sixteenth century, and were not revived until the European scramble for Africa in the 1800s.

With the Virgin Mary and the child Jesus, identified by the cross round his neck, perched triumphantly on the lid, and snakes festooning the base, the ivory appears to be a graphic image of good overcoming evil. Though the use of snakes to symbolize evil has strong roots in the Hebrew Bible, Jesus himself didn't seek to externalize or personalize the evil from which he had come to save people. Rather, he implies that he has come to challenge people's shortcomings, their insufficient faith, their half-hearted love. That would be much harder to deal with.

Ivory, Benin, Nigeria, 15th century

CHURCH

THE FIRST AND THIRTEENTH APOSTLES

Jesus chose his group of disciples to ensure that his message had a continuing life. Their leader, Peter, comes across as a rather unstable character, who misses the point as often as he grasps it. But he led the preaching at Pentecost and could heal in Jesus' name. He became convinced that Christ's saving mission was for all humanity, not just for Jews.

He was martyred in Rome, it was believed, in AD 64. The church in Rome gradually came to use Christ's promise to Peter: 'On this rock I will build my church', as the key to its own authority. When Rome lost political power, the bishops of Rome retained this moral authority, particularly with the new churches of western Europe, and on this the claims of papal primacy are based.

Saul had not known Jesus in life but, more than any other individual, was to ensure Christianity's survival. He first appears in the New Testament persecuting Christians, but his encounter with Christ on the road to Damascus was radically to change all that. This spectacular maiolica plate is so crowded with characters and scenery that it is quite hard to identify Saul at all. He saw a light in the sky and heard Jesus' voice; falling from his horse, he was blinded for several days. For Paul, as he was afterwards known, this was as powerful an experience as if he had met Jesus in the flesh.

After this, Paul travelled unsparingly, bringing people to Christ throughout the eastern Mediterranean. Through his letters to these new Christian communities, he has become the principal expounder of mainstream Christian theology and the organization of the church.

Previous page: 12th century wall-paintings at the church of Lagoudhera, Cyprus

Maiolica, probably from Urbino or Venice, Italy, around 1540

THE TRANSMISSION OF THE BIBLE

Jesus himself, like most religious leaders of the ancient world, left no writings at all. Paul's letters to the earliest Christian communities, founded as the result of his preaching around the Mediterranean, are the earliest Christian texts to survive. The earliest probably dates from *c.* AD 50, less than twenty years after Jesus' crucifixion. The four gospel accounts of Jesus' life, death and teaching were written a generation or so later. Together with the Acts of the Apostles, an account of the early church in Jerusalem and the missionary journeys of Paul, various other epistles and the concluding Book of Revelation, the twenty-seven books which came to form the New Testament were gradually accepted as canonical during the late second and early third century. The Hebrew Bible, the contents of which had been agreed by Jews by the second century BC, was taken up by Christians as the Old Testament.

No doubt because it had come into existence to satisfy the demands of worshippers, the Bible remained central to Christian worship and as a tool of Christian mission. About a century after Christianity arrived in Anglo-Saxon England, the Anglo-Saxons produced this magnificent version of the four gospels, illuminated in the monastery on Lindisfarne by the artist-scribe Eadfrith. It is written in Latin, but there is an inter-leaving of Anglo-Saxon within the lines, added in the tenth century, although the principle of translating the scriptures into the vernacular was not to become common practice until the Reformation.

Manuscript page from the Lindisfarne Gospels, Northumbria, 7th century

INCIPIT EUANGELIUM SECUNDUM MATTHEU

cristes

uutedlice
ƿuæs þæs
cristes cneu
reð ro

godlice

XPI AUTEM GENE

cynn ƿæccenise t cneuriƿu   ƿuæs ður   þus   mid ðy

RATIO XPI ERAT CVM

þus   bi poeðdes t beboden t beƿeaƿnuð t betaht

 togemanne
nalles to hab
banne sþif

ESSET DESPONSATA

moder   his

MATER EIUS MARIC IOSEPH

abiachan
ðe aldormon þær indæm
tid in hieru
ralem pone
hycob he he be
beod maria
ioræphe to
gemenne y
tobægeong
annt mid
claennisse

TRANSMISSION OF ICONS

What did Jesus look like? What – or who – should he have looked like? If he was God, as his followers believed, was it not blasphemous to try to show what he looked like at all?

As the Christian community grew, there was an insatiable demand for visual material, on tombs and sarcophagi, on personal jewellery, on objects used in worship, as decoration in books and on the walls of churches. More than illustrations, these images, 'icons' in Greek, were aids to worship, prompters of faith. To be reliable in this role, they had to be in some sense a 'true' likeness, which usually meant being derived from an existing, tried-and-tested image. So a body of images grew which were canonical, like the biblical text.

This icon invokes Orthodox beliefs about icons at several different periods of Christian history. The icon-within-an-icon, around which everyone is grouped, is a classic version of the Virgin and Child, as the *Hodegetria*, 'pointing the way'. It was kept in Constantinople for centuries, and even had its own monastery named after it. The surrounding group are historical characters of the ninth century, when the use of icons was restored after a period of Iconoclasm, during which existing sacred art was destroyed and no new examples were made. The icon itself dates from the fifteenth century, when it may have been painted as a protective measure, when the Orthodox Christian city of Constantinople was under threat from both the Latin West and the Muslim Turks.

Icon, Constantinople (modern Istanbul, Turkey), early 15th century

BAPTISM

John the Baptist had said of Jesus, 'I baptize you with water, but he will baptize you with the Holy Spirit and with fire'. Despite this reference to the experience of Pentecost, entrance to the Christian community from its earliest days was by baptism with water. Three thousand were baptized at Pentecost itself.

During the early centuries this was adult baptism, usually carried out by a bishop, the leader of the local community, on the main feasts of the Christian year, principally at Easter. Early churches had a special walk-through baptistery, often octagonal in shape. But as Christianity spread through the population of the Roman world, the rite changed to infant baptism, so that a child could be brought up in the church. At the Reformation, however, groups such as the Anabaptists reasserted the practice of adult baptism, so as to stress that baptism is an act of personal rather than communal confession of faith.

Whether for child or adult, baptism remains a very communal experience, so this is a particularly rare treasure: the only known example in England of a gold font made for private use. It was commissioned by the third duke of Portland for the christening of his first grandson in 1796; designed by Humphrey Repton, better known for his gardens, and made by the workshop of Paul Storr, one of the most celebrated London goldsmiths. The figures are Faith, standing holding a cross, Hope with an anchor and Charity, appropriately nursing children.

Gold, London, 1797-8

EUCHARIST

Jesus may not have instituted the sacrament of baptism, but his actions at the Last Supper ensured that whenever his followers ate or drank together they remembered his sacrificial death. The church soon developed their shared meal, or *agape*, into the eucharist, the central act of Christian worship. A eucharistic meal is shown in the Roman catacomb paintings, and a fourth-century silver chalice from Water Newton in Roman Britain is part of the earliest known set of liturgical plate.

This lacquer *pyx*, used to hold the bread for the eucharist, was made in late sixteenth-century Japan in the *makie* technique, painting with gold or silver dust. The lid is a European addition: *IHS*, the first three letters of Jesus' name in Greek, was taken up as the monogram of the Jesuits, the Society of Jesus. Their first missionaries to Japan, from around 1550, were very successful and by about 1600 they had around 750,000 converts. But the Jesuits were not trusted by their fellow-Christians, and they could not ordain Japanese priests to make the mission self-sufficient. The Japanese government outlawed Christianity in 1614; by the 1650s some 5000 Christians had been put to death, and the mission totally extinguished.

The eucharist itself has not always been the sacrament of unity which Christians claim. Differences over whether Christ is really present in the bread and wine divided Catholics and Protestants at the Reformation, and differences about the role of the eucharist in building up or expressing the fullness of life in Christ still cause division to this day.

Lacquer, Japan, late 16th – early 17th century

DISCIPLESHIP

CHRISTIAN SOLDIERS

Military analogies for human behaviour spring easily to the tongue. Paul popularized the concept of the Christian soldier, urging people to put on the armour of God and fight the good fight. Erasmus, the sixteenth-century humanist, used the same analogy in his *Handbook of the Christian Soldier*. The civilian saints on this ivory triptych were probably just as heroic in their sanctity as their military colleagues, George, Theodore Stratelates and Eustachius, about whom little is actually known. The military theme is further reinforced on the outside leaves by monograms of Christ's name with the Greek *NIKA*, victory.

The question of whether a Christian should actually take up arms has exercised people since Jesus' own lifetime. Jesus' resistance to his third temptation, of power-seeking, perhaps leading a Jewish independence movement against Rome, has been suggested as the cause of Judas' disillusionment. Some have concluded that a leader who urged his followers to turn the other cheek, and told Peter at Gethsemane to abjure violence, demands a pacifist response. But Jesus also said 'I have come not to bring peace but a sword', and threw the money lenders out of the Temple.

Constantine after his conversion in AD 312 required Christians to serve in the Roman army – he even painted the *chi-rho* monogram on his soldiers' shields. Medieval Christianity is notorious for its Crusades against Islamic regimes, unconverted northern tribes and even Christian heretics. However, in modern times the right of conscientious objection to military service has become widely respected, and some Christians are now extending this by refusing to pay taxes for military expenditure.

Previous page: Basilica church at Qa'lat Siman, Syria, built over the site where St Simeon spent thirty-seven years standing on a pillar

Ivory, Constantinople (modern Istanbul, Turkey), 10th century

SUFFERING FOR CHRIST

Throughout Christianity, especially in the Catholic tradition, the experience of the Crucifixion has served to mark the extremity of Christ's identification with humanity and human suffering. By meditating on the Crucifixion, worshippers strive to reach the heart of the mystery of the Incarnation.

This belief has given rise to extreme physical manifestations, such as the stigmata, the marks of the five wounds of Christ, which have appeared apparently spontaneously on Christians from St Francis of Assisi in the thirteenth century to the Cappuchin priest Padre Pio in the twentieth century. The visual equivalent has given rise to such master-pieces as Matthias Grünewald's Isenheim altarpiece, painted for a monastic hospital chapel near Colmar, in Alsace.

At much the same period, the owner of this late fifteenth-century ring could meditate on the five wounds, described as the wells of pity, mercy, comfort, grace and everlasting life. This ring may also have had an apotropaic significance, to ward off evil. The inscription inside, also incorporating the names of the three Magi, a charm against epilepsy and one of the ten names of God, reads:

> 'The five wounds of Christ are my medicine
> the Cross and Passion of Christ are my medicine
> Jasper Melchior Balthazar anazapta tetragrammata'

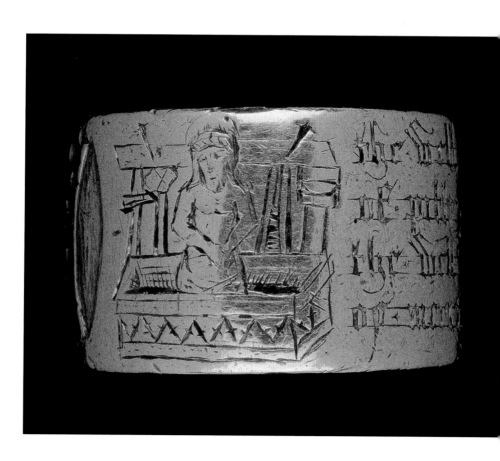

Gold, London, late 15th century

LOVE OF CHRIST

Your love is more fragrant than wine
Fragrant is the scent of your anointing oils
and your name is like those oils poured out
that is why maidens love you

Song of Songs

The opening lines of the Song of Songs, an erotic dialogue between bride and bridegroom in the Hebrew Bible, show that sexual imagery for the response of the soul to God has a long history in the Judaeo-Christian tradition. In Christianity, this was extended to include the concept of the whole church as the bride of Christ.

St Agnes is one of many women in the early church who refused marriage for love of Christ. As a punishment, she was imprisoned in a brothel. When her disappointed bridegroom Procopius was strangled by a demon she restored him to life, but she was nevertheless sentenced to death by burning. The flames had no effect on her, and finally she had to be put to death with a spear.

These scenes appear on the cover and bowl of this majestic gold cup, decorated with translucent enamels and pearls. The cup has been in the royal treasuries of both France, where it was a gift from the duc de Berry to his uncle Charles VI, and of England, where the roses were added to the stem of the cup – the dynastic Tudor rose, rather than the rose of Sharon of the Song of Songs!

Gold and enamel, France, late 14th century

SEEING CHRIST IN OTHERS

Jesus opened his ministry in the synagogue of his home town of Nazareth by preaching on the text from Isaiah:

> He has sent me to announce good news to the poor
> to proclaim release for prisoners
> and recovery of sight for the blind
> to let the broken victims go free
> to proclaim the year of the Lord's favour

Luke 4.18

'Today', he said, 'in your hearing, this text has come true'. In an even more vivid image, in conversations before his death, he anticipated what God would ask of people at the Last Judgement: 'When I was hungry, did you give me food?' and the punchline, 'Anything you did for one of my brothers, however insignificant, you did for me'. (Matthew 25.40)

This medal takes up the clearest expression of Christ's theme of love of neighbour, which comes in the collection of his preaching known as the Sermon on the Mount (Matthew 7.12). Some of the strongest movements for social justice have had Christian inspiration – the Jubilee 2000 campaign for third world debt remission drew through Luke on Isaiah and Leviticus in the Old Testament. The anti-slavery movement was similarly motivated, as this medal makes clear. The Society for the Abolition of the Slave Trade, which issued these medals, was founded in 1787, at a time when 60,000 slaves per year were being carried across the Atlantic from West Africa to the Americas. With Christian support from liberal sects including the Quakers and evangelicals such as William Wilberforce, slavery was eventually abolished throughout British territories in 1833.

Brass, London, around 1787

WHATSOEVER
YE WOULD THAT
MEN SHOULD DO
TO YOU, DO YE
EVEN SO TO
THEM.

SEEING CHRIST IN CREATION

The idea that the whole of creation expresses Christ has taken a longer time to develop. So this silver brooch, made in Anglo-Saxon England in the late ninth century, possibly in Alfred the Great's court workshop, is far ahead of its time. It encompasses all the created world: the roundels in each quadrant show human, animal, bird and plant motifs, and in the centre are figures representing the five senses with which humans appreciate nature (from top right): smell, touch, hearing and taste, with sight at the centre. The eyes of the mind lead to wisdom, Greek *sophia*, often seen in the Middle Ages as an attribute of Christ.

Jesus used plant and animal imagery lavishly in his ministry – for instance, the lilies of the field, 'not even Solomon in all his glory was arrayed like one of these', and the sparrow, which does not fall to earth without God's notice. But it is illustrative rather than didactic, and Christianity has preferred the version in Genesis, where the natural world is provided for the sustenance of humanity, and man has dominion over it. Isaiah's images of the peaceable kingdom, though strengthened by the classical Orphic tradition, have also failed to take deep root in mainstream Christianity.

There are signs of activity, now, especially in the Orthodox Churches who are working closely with the World Wildlife Fund, that this long lacuna in Christian thought may be starting to be filled. In turn this may perhaps help to inspire new iconographical forms of expression.

Silver, England, 9th century

Churchyard at Bushey, Hertfordshire, pen and ink drawing with watercolour by William Henry Hunt, 1822; his patron Dr Thomas Munro is shown on horseback at the right, and one of the tombs is that of Munro's son Henry.

HEAVEN

INEVITABILITY OF DEATH

The second of Jesus' temptations was to dice with death, in the expectation that God would send angels to save him. He rejected this, and he did the same in the Garden of Gethsemane, when he struggled with the natural desire to avoid his forthcoming death to a willingness to embrace it. It is at the centre of Christian faith that God in Jesus has endured this most bitter of human experiences: not only death itself, but the fear of death.

Poised on the brink of the Reformation, the artist, draughtsman and engraver Albrecht Dürer created the definitive image for this, as for so many other aspects of the Christian life. Death surrounds the knight: it is the skull at his horse's feet and the corpse holding an hour-glass before his eyes. The city set on a hill in the distance seems very far away.

'For none of us lives, and equally none of us dies, for himself alone. If we live, we live for the Lord, and if we die, we die for the Lord. So whether we live or die, we belong to the Lord'. (Romans 14.7)

Knight, Death and the Devil, copperplate engraving, Albrecht Dürer, Germany, 1513

THE LAST JUDGEMENT

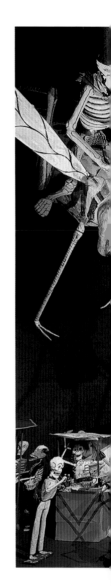

Jesus appears to have believed that there would be a future reckoning, and that he would return in glory: many of the parables use such images as the master of the house returning, and holding people to account. Before this, though, there would be a time of trial, and devastation would come upon the world. There are apocalyptic passages in all the gospels, but it is the Book of Revelation which goes to the greatest lengths to expound the sequence of events of the 'last days'.

Among the most famous Revelation images is that of the Four Horsemen: Conquest, War, Famine and Death, 'and Hell followed close behind'. European art is full of these images, most famously that of Dürer's print of 1498, and the imagery is still being reworked in modern fiction and cinema, in works such as Francis Ford Coppola's *Apocalypse Now* (1979).

But the Mexican artists of *The Day of the Dead* use this imagery of skull and skeleton in a very different way, as a joyful celebration of the interrelationship of life and death. The Linares family of Mexico City made their four life-size papier-mâché horsemen as part of a large-scale work of 132 pieces called *The Atomic Apocalypse*. It includes specific references to well-known historical atrocities and ongoing conflicts, but still treats this terrifying material with a cartoon-like approach.

The Day of the Dead, papier-mâché, Mexico City, 1983

90

RESURRECTION FOR ALL

Christians have found it hard to comprehend the promise of the Resurrection. Is it really being offered to all? Does it depend on what one did in life, can it be earned? Or is it a free gift from God? Can God really be that prodigal? The problem is summed up in the human response to the parable of the Prodigal Son: we are thankful for the return of the repentant wrongdoer, but feel more than a twinge of sympathy for the elder brother: 'you never slaughtered the fatted calf for me!'

Another problem is the sheer scale of the numbers of the dead. As the Book of Revelation has it: 'I looked and saw a vast throng, which no one could count, from all races and tribes, nations and languages, standing before the throne and the Lamb' (Revelation 7.9). How can God possibly discriminate between all these souls, even with Jesus at his right hand?

Resurrection visual imagery has swung between the massed ranks of great Last Judgements like that of the Sistine Chapel, and the homely touch of the local worthies of Cookham emerging from their graves as visualized by Stanley Spencer. This magnificent reliquary has elements of both. It was made for Jean duc de Berry, brother of the French king and patron of the famous illuminated manuscripts, the Très Riches Heures. Created to house a single thorn from Christ's crown of thorns, the main scene shows Christ in Majesty, and below, clothed in white enamel, are the souls emerging from their graves, 'shining like the sun in the kingdom of their Father' (Matthew 13.43).

Gold, enamel and precious stones, France, late 14th century

HEAVEN ON EARTH

In describing life with Christ, we are at the limits of human visual and verbal imagery. The Book of Revelation describes the enduring City of God: its towering walls, streets of gold, jewelled gates. But the promise only touches the heart when it echoes our deepest experiences: 'He will wipe every tear from their eyes. There shall be an end to death, and to mourning and crying and pain' (Revelation 21.4).

But could Heaven ever come on earth, either in this life or after Christ's return in glory? Christianity has a strong apocalyptic tradition of identifying historical events in this world with the account in Revelation. The great cartoonist James Gillray caricatured one of these episodes, when Richard Brothers, a former seaman turned prophet, identified the final Apocalypse with the French Revolution. Here Brothers tramples on the Beast of Revelation as he leads a group of Jews to rebuild Jerusalem, carrying on his back a 'bundle of the elect' which includes the pro-French Whig politician Charles James Fox.

Around him London landmarks such as St. Paul's crash in ruins. Francis Thompson also sets his *The Kingdom of God* in London, but offers a more optimistic vision of Heaven on earth:

> But (when so sad thou canst not sadder)
> Cry; – and upon thy so sore loss
> Shall shine the traffic of Jacob's ladder
> Pitched twixt Heaven and Charing Cross
>
> Yea, in the night, my Soul, my daughter,
> Cry, – clinging Heaven by the hems;
> and lo, Christ walking on the water,
> Not of Genesareth, but Thames!

Etching, hand-coloured, James Gillray, London, 1795

FURTHER READING

Apostolos-Cappadona, D., *Dictionary of Women in Religious Art*, Oxford, 1998
Davie, D., *New Oxford Book of Christian Verse*, Oxford, 1988
Drury, J., *Painting the Word: Christian Pictures and their Meanings*, New Haven, 2002
Dyrness, W. A., *Visual Faith: Art, Theology and Worship in Dialogue (Engaging Culture)*, Michigan, 2001
Gilmore Holt, E., *A Documentary History of Art*, (vol. I), New Jersey, 1982
Grabar, A., *Christian Iconography: A Study of its Origins*, New Jersey, 1968
Hastings, A., ed., *A World History of Christianity*, Michigan, 1999
MacGregor, N., *Seeing Salvation: Images of Christ in Art*, New Haven and London, 2000
Murray, P., and Murray, L., *Oxford Companion to Christian Art and Architecture*, Oxford, 1998
Williams, R., *The Dwelling of the Light: Praying with Icons of Christ*, Norwich, 2003

ILLUSTRATION REFERENCES

British Museum objects (indicated BM) are © The Trustees of The British Museum and are courtesy of the Department of Photography and Imaging.

page	
2	BM, P&D 1895 9-15-655
6	BM, M&ME 1955 5-7-1
9	BM, M&ME 1965 4-9 1
11	BM, OA 1919 1-1 0.48
13	BM, C&M 1992 1-13 4634
14-15	BM, P&D 1928 3-10 100
17	BM, M&ME 1919 3-5 1
19	BM, M&ME 1885 8-4 4
21	BM, M&ME 1852 3-27 10
23	BM, M&ME 1922 4-12 2
25	BM, M&ME 1974 10-2 1
27	BM, M&ME 1839 10-39 43
29	BM, M&ME 1856 6-23 20
31	BM, P&D 1973 U 1022
33	BM, M&ME 1852 1-2 2
35	BM, M&ME 1981 7-1 1-13
37	BM, M&ME 1856 6-23 4
39	BM, M&ME 1855 3-5 1
41	BM, M&ME 1905 5-22 1
43	BM, M&ME 1902 5-29 24
45	BM, M&ME 1983 7-4 1
47	British Library MS Yates Thompson 4 f.35
48-9	Photograph by Rowena Loverance

page	
51	BM, M&ME 1856 7-18 1
53	BM, M&ME 1854 6-5 1
54-5	BM, M&ME 1867 1-20 1
57	BM, P&D M-88-25
59	BM, M&ME 1908 3-6 1
61	BM, Ethno 1981 Af 35 1a, b
62-3	Photograph by Rowena Loverance
65	BM, M&ME 1885 4-20 2
67	British Library MS Cotton Nero D. IV f.29
69	BM, M&ME 1988 4-11 1
71	BM, M&ME 1986 4-3 1
73	BM, OA 1969 4-15 1a,b
74-5	Photograph Rowena Loverance
77	BM, M&ME 1923 12-5 1
79	BM, M&ME AF 897
81	BM, M&ME 1892 5-1 1
83	BM, C&M Banks NJC 148
85	BM, M&ME 1952 4-4 1
86-7	BM, P&D 1921 7-14 14
89	BM, P&D 1868 8-22 198
91	BM, Ethno Study Collection
93	BM, M&ME Wadd.67
95	BM, P&D 1868 8-8 6470